Peanuts at School

Other PEANUTS albums available
from Hodder and Stoughton:

The Peanuts Gang
Snoopy Classics
The Snoopy Festival
Snoopy Parade
Snoopy Treasury
You're a Good Scout, Snoopy

Peanuts at School

Charles M. Schulz

HODDER AND STOUGHTON
LONDON SYDNEY AUCKLAND TORONTO

British Library Cataloguing in Publication Data

Schulz, Charles M.
Peanuts at School
I. Title
741.5'973   PN6727.53
ISBN 0-340-35391-0

First published in 1982 by Holt, Rinehart and Winston, New York
under the title CLASSROOM PEANUTS
First published in Great Britain 1984

Published by Hodder and Stoughton Children's Books,
a division of Hodder and Stoughton Ltd,
Mill Road, Dunton Green, Sevenoaks, Kent TN13 2YJ

Printed in Belgium by Henri Proost & Cie, Turnhout

YES, MA'AM... I'M READY..

THIS IS "SHOW AND TELL" TIME...

FOR ALL YOU LUCKY KIDS OUT THERE IN CLASSROOM-LAND I'VE BROUGHT MY FAMOUS LEAF COLLECTION!

BUT FIRST, A WORD FROM MY SPONSOR..

THESE LEAVES ARE BROUGHT TO YOU THROUGH THE COURTESY OF OUR COUNTRY'S TREES

MY LEAF COLLECTION WAS GATHERED FROM MANY LAWNS AND ALONGSIDE MANY CURBS... THESE ARE LEAVES FROM ALL WALKS OF LIFE...

AND NOW A BRIEF WORD FROM MY CO-SPONSOR, THE RAIN...

THE RAIN COMES DOWN FROM THE CLOUDS WHICH ARE IN THE SKY, AND WATERS THE SOIL UPON WHICH SIT THE TREES WHEREON GREW THESE LEAVES...

WHICH BRINGS US BACK TO MY FAMOUS COLLECTION.. YES, MA'AM?

FIRST THEY WANT YOU TO SHOW AND TELL, AND THEN THEY DON'T WANT YOU TO SHOW AND TELL...

I KNOW THE ANSWER! I KNOW THE ANSWER!

THE ANSWER IS TWELVE!

IT ISN'T?

SIXTEEN? NINE? FORTY-TWO? ONE?

HOW WOULD IT BE IF I JUST SPELLED MISSISSIPPI?

SEVEN O'CLOCK, SALLY... TIME TO GET UP!

GOOD GRIEF... I'VE GOT TO HURRY...

The Incas

The Incas were people who lived a long time ago in Incaland.

They had a highly developed civilization.

They would still be here today, but they lacked motel facilities.

SOME OF MY BEST TERM PAPERS HAVE BEEN WRITTEN BEFORE BREAKFAST!

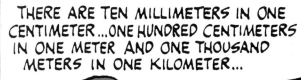

SO IT'S "SHOW AND TELL" TIME AGAIN, IS IT? WELL, DO I EVER HAVE A SURPRISE FOR YOU TODAY!

I HAVE A LITTLE FILM TO SHOW YOU THAT'S GONNA KNOCK YOUR EYES OUT!

NO, MA'AM... THAT'S ONLY AN EXPRESSION..

ALL RIGHT, IF I CAN HAVE A COUPLE OF YOU STRONG TYPES LIFT THIS PROJECTOR INTO PLACE, WE CAN GET THIS SHOW ON THE ROAD!

NO, LET'S PUT IT ON THAT TABLE BACK THERE... HOW ABOUT YOU FOUR WEIRDOS MOVING THAT TABLE?

AND I'LL NEED A COUPLE MORE TO PUT THIS SCREEN UP... LET'S GO!! ON THE DOUBLE, THERE!

STRETCH THAT CORD ACROSS THE BACK, AND PLUG IT INTO THAT SOCKET IN THE CORNER...

OKAY, SOMEONE RUN DOWN TO THE CUSTODIAN THEN, AND GET AN EXTENSION! YOU THERE, GET GOING!!

NOW, WHAT ABOUT THOSE WINDOW SHADES? LET'S HAVE ALL OF YOU WHO SIT ALONG THE SIDE THERE PULL DOWN THOSE STUPID SHADES..

AND I'LL NEED SOMEONE ON THE LIGHT SWITCH... ONE VOLUNTEER... YOU THERE, HONEY, GET THE SWITCH!

IS THAT THE BELL ALREADY?

OKAY, WE'LL TAKE IT TOMORROW FROM HERE.. EVERYONE BE IN PLACE BY NINE! THANK YOU, AND GOOD MORNING!

Theme: Our School

Going to our school is an education in itself which is not to be confused with actually getting an education.

I DON'T NEED THAT KIND OF TROUBLE!

THIS IS AN ARTICLE I'VE WRITTEN FOR SCHOOL CALLED "WILD ANIMALS OF THE WEST"

"THERE ARE MANY WILD ANIMALS WHO LIVE IN THE WEST..SOME WHO LIVE IN THE MOUNTAINS ARE CALLED MOUNTAIN LIONS..."

"NOW, OF COURSE, WHERE YOU HAVE MOUNTAINS, YOU HAVE GULLIES... THE WILD ANIMALS WHO LIVE IN THE GULLIES ARE CALLED...."

"... GULLY CATS "?

THE TITLE OF MY ESSAY IS, "WILD ANIMALS OF THE WEST"

OUT WEST THERE ARE MANY GULLIES AND THESE GULLIES ARE FILLED WITH GULLY CATS... GULLY CATS ARE EXTREMELY FIERCE...

IN FACT, ONE OF THE MOST COMMON OF WESTERN SAYINGS IS THE ONE THAT GOES...

"NEVER GRIEVE A GULLY CAT!"

AND THEN I READ MY PAPER ON GULLY CATS TO THE WHOLE CLASS..

I TOLD ALL ABOUT HOW FIERCE GULLY CATS ARE, AND I EVEN THREW IN A BIT ABOUT HOW THEY ARE IMMUNE TO THE BITE OF THE DREADED QUEEN SNAKE

WHAT SORT OF A GRADE DID YOUR TEACHER GIVE YOU?

" NICE TRY "

THOSE DREAMS I HAVE AT NIGHT ARE GOING TO DRIVE ME CRAZY

LAST NIGHT I DREAMED THAT LITTLE RED-HAIRED GIRL AND I WERE EATING LUNCH TOGETHER...

BUT SHE'S GONE..SHE'S MOVED AWAY, AND I DON'T KNOW WHERE SHE LIVES, AND SHE DOESN'T KNOW I EVEN EXIST, AND I'LL NEVER SEE HER AGAIN...AND...

I WISH MEN CRIED..

DUCK, BIG BROTHER! HERE COMES ANOTHER DAY!!

WE ALL NEED HOPE, FRANKLIN, DID YOU KNOW THAT?

AND WE ALL NEED MEMORIES... WITHOUT GOOD MEMORIES, LIFE CAN BE PRETTY SKUNGIE...

I HAD THREE GOOD MEMORIES ONCE...

BUT I FORGOT WHAT THEY WERE!

I'M STILL HUNGRY..

I ATE A PEANUT BUTTER SANDWICH, AN APPLE AND TWO COOKIES, BUT I'M STILL HUNGRY..

THAT ALWAYS USED TO BE ENOUGH FOR ME..

TRASH

I THINK I'VE OUTGROWN MY LUNCH!

This report is on sheepherders.

Sheepherders raise lambs from which we get lambchops.

They also raise sheep from which we get sheepchops.

SHEEPCHOPS?

HOW ABOUT A GAME OF MARBLES AFTER SCHOOL, FRANKLIN?

I CAN'T..I HAVE A GUITAR LESSON AT THREE-THIRTY...

RIGHT AFTER THAT I HAVE LITTLE LEAGUE, AND THEN SWIM CLUB, AND THEN DINNER AND THEN A '4 H' MEETING

I LEAD A VERY ACTIVE TUESDAY!

Ten milligrams equals one centigram.

Ten decigrams equals one gram.

Ten grams equals one grampa.

KEEP GOING... I CAN HARDLY WAIT TO SEE WHAT COMES NEXT...

I'M DOOMED!

I HAVE TO WRITE A REPORT ON RIVERS AND IT'S DUE NEXT WEEK, AND I JUST KNOW I'LL GET A FAILING GRADE!

WHY DON'T YOU WORK REAL HARD AND TURN IN THE BEST REPORT THAT YOU CAN POSSIBLY WRITE?

THAT NEVER OCCURRED TO ME!

This is the last English theme of the year, and it is a good thing.

What a waste these themes are. What a drag. What a bummer.

THAT'S PROBABLY NOT A GOOD IDEA...

This is my theme on Memorial Day which I am writing on Monday because there is no school today.

Everyone is observing Memorial Day today so they can have a three-day weekend and go water skiing.

Which hasn't much to do with Memorial Day which is really tomorrow.

THIS IS THE SORT THEME WHERE YOU GET EITHER AN "A" OR AN "F"!

TRUE! FALSE! TRUE!

TRUE! FALSE! FALSE! TRUE! FALSE! FALSE! TRUE! FALSE!

TRUE! FALSE! TRUE! TRUE! FALSE! TRUE! TRUE! TRUE! TRUE! FALSE! TRUE! FALSE!

AND ONE GOOD OLD FASHIONED **MAYBE**!!

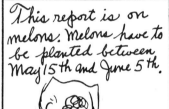

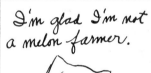

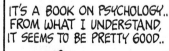

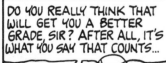

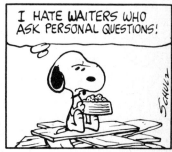

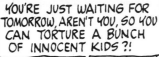

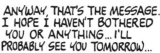

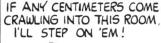

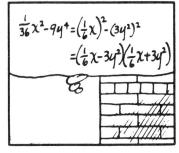

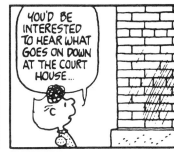

DOT DOT DOT DOT DOT DOT DOT DOT

THIS IS A SCHOOL PROJECT.. I'M DRAWING A MAP OF THE WHOLE WORLD...

I HAVE TO PUT IN ALL THE COUNTRIES, AND ALL THE CAPITALS, AND ALL THE MOUNTAINS, AND THE RIVERS, AND THE TREES, AND THE ROCKS AND ALL THE PEOPLE!

DOT DOT DOT DOT DOT DOT DOT DOT DOT DOT DOT

THIS IS THE HARDEST PART.. DRAWING IN ALL THEIR EYES...

I'M ALSO PUTTING IN ALL THE DOGS AND CATS AND BUGS..DO YOU REALIZE HOW MANY BUGS THERE ARE IN THE WORLD?

THERE! IT'S FINISHED! NOW, I CAN GO TO BED KNOWING IT'S BEEN A JOB WELL DONE...

SHE SURE GETS INVOLVED IN SOME WEIRD PROJECTS

DOT DOT DOT DOT DOT DOT DOT DOT

I THOUGHT YOU WERE IN BED...I THOUGHT YOU WERE FINISHED...

I FORGOT HORSES AND COWS...

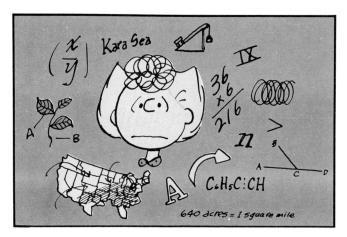

QUESTION NUMBER ONE...
WHAT IS THE CAPITAL OF
CAMEROUN?

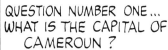

Answer: When I grow up, I
am going to be a hair dresser,
and hair dressers obviously
don't have to know such things.

QUESTION NUMBER TWO...
WHAT IS THE LENGTH OF
THE RIO GRANDE RIVER?

Answer: When I grow up, I will
also probably be a housewife, and
could not care less about the length
of the Rio Grande river.

QUESTION NUMBER THREE... WHAT IS THE
NAME OF THE LARGEST PYRAMID?

Answer: When I grow
up, I will undoubtedly
be a member of the smart set.

We members of the smart set
rarely discuss such things
as pyramids.

THIS IS AN
EASY TEST..

FOR MY NATURE REPORT TODAY, I AM BRINGING YOU AN EXCLUSIVE!

ROCK SNAKES!!

WHAT, YOU MAY ASK, IS A ROCK SNAKE? THAT IS A GOOD QUESTION! A ROCK SNAKE IS A SNAKE THAT SNEAKS UP BEHIND YOU, AND THROWS A ROCK AT YOU!

NOW, HERE IS MY EXCLUSIVE....IT USED TO BE THOUGHT THAT ROCK SNAKES WERE DANGEROUS, BUT MY AUTHORITY SAYS THIS IS NOT SO...

A ROCK SNAKE CANNOT THROW VERY HIGH, YOU SEE, SO THEREFORE, ALL HE CAN DO IS HIT YOU ON THE BACK OF THE LEG....SO SAYS MY AUTHORITY!

MA'AM?

LINUS VAN PELT.... YES, MA'AM..

SHE SAID SHE REMEMBERS YOU FROM WHEN YOU WERE IN HER CLASS!

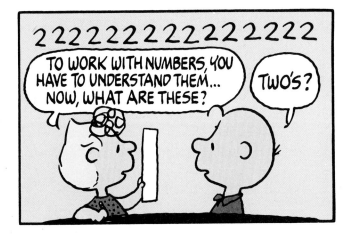

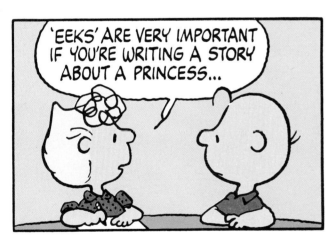

Deer

THAT SHOULD BE "DEAR"

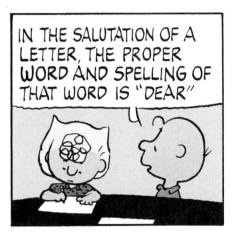

IN THE SALUTATION OF A LETTER, THE PROPER WORD AND SPELLING OF THAT WORD IS "DEAR"

Deer are beautiful animals found in most parts of the world.

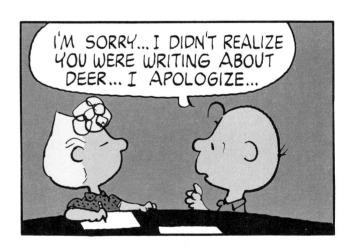

I'M SORRY... I DIDN'T REALIZE YOU WERE WRITING ABOUT DEER... I APOLOGIZE...

WELL, I SHOULD HOPE SO! IT SEEMS TO ME THAT A LOT OF THE PROBLEMS IN THIS WORLD ARE CAUSED BY PEOPLE WHO CRITICIZE OTHER PEOPLE BEFORE THEY KNOW WHAT THEY'RE TALKING ABOUT!

Dear Grandma,

WHAT KIND OF A REPORT CARD DO YOU CALL THIS?

I DIDN'T EVEN GET ANY GRADES...

ALL IT SAYS IS, "GOOD HUSTLE!"

FOR "SHOW AND TELL" TODAY I HAVE BROUGHT YOU A LOCAL HERO!

THIS LITTLE FELLOW HERE BROKE HIS FIFTH METATARSAL WHILE RESCUING THREE AIRLINE STEWARDESSES ON RUNAWAY HORSES!

LISTEN CAREFULLY, FOR THIS IS THE WAY IT ALL HAPPENED...

INCIDENTALLY, MA'AM, ARE WE GRADED ON TRUTH AND ACCURACY?

FOR "SHOW AND TELL" I BRING YOU THE TALE OF A HERO...

YOU REALIZE, OF COURSE, I'M NOT BRINGING HIS TAIL...HE BROUGHT HIS OWN TAIL...WHAT I'M BRINGING IS HIS TALE! YOU KNOW WHAT I MEAN?

BOOT!

OKAY....ON WITH THE STORY...

TO BEGIN OUR STORY WE MUST GO BACK SEVERAL YEARS...

WE MUST GO BACK TO THE CHILDHOOD YEARS OF OUR THREE AIRLINE STEWARDESSES, EVELYN, PAT AND SHIRLEY...

EVELYN WAS BORN IN MISSOURI, PAT IN WISCONSIN AND SHIRLEY IN PENNSYLVANIA... NOW, WHEN EVELYN WAS ONLY THIRTEEN, SHE...

I'M SORRY, MA'AM...YES, I UNDERSTAND...WELL, JUST HOW MUCH TIME DO WE HAVE?

..AN' THAT'S THE END OF OUR HERO'S STORY!

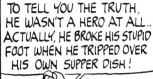

TO TELL YOU THE TRUTH, HE WASN'T A HERO AT ALL.. ACTUALLY, HE BROKE HIS STUPID FOOT WHEN HE TRIPPED OVER HIS OWN SUPPER DISH!

THIS CONCLUDES OUR PORTION OF "SHOW AND TELL"

WE NOW SWITCH YOU BACK TO YOUR LOCAL STATIONS!

Dear Pen Pal,

It has been a long time since I have written to you.

Things are pretty much the same around here

Especially my penmanship!

Dear Pen Pal,
Today I am going to try to write you a neat letter.

No smudges and no smears

LOOK AT THAT! YOU SMEARED "SMUDGE," AND YOU SMUDGED "SMEAR"! THAT'S VERY FUNNY! DON'T YOU THINK THAT'S FUNNY?

I THOUGHT IT WAS VERY FUNNY!

A NEW SCHOOL!! WOW!

I DIDN'T THINK THEY'D EVER GET YOU BUILT! I SUPPOSE YOU HEARD THAT OUR LAST SCHOOL HAD A NERVOUS BREAKDOWN

ONE DAY HE JUST COLLAPSED! I THINK HE WAS TOO SENSITIVE... ✻ SIGH ✻

FIRST DAY ON THE JOB, I RUN INTO A WEIRDO!

I THINK I SHOULD WARN YOU

AS A SCHOOL, YOU SHOULD BE PREPARED FOR A LOT OF CRITICISM... THEY'RE GOING TO CURSE AND REVILE YOU!

YOU'LL BE FALSELY ACCUSED... YOU'LL ALSO BE VANDALIZED, PLUNDERED AND SABOTAGED!

I WANNA GO HOME!

YES, MA'AM.. THIS YEAR I PLAN TO GET NOTHING BUT STRAIGHT A'S!

THAT DOESN'T MEAN, OF COURSE, THAT I WOULDN'T ACCEPT A FEW BENT ONES...

HAHAHAHA!

YES, MA'AM

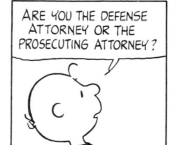

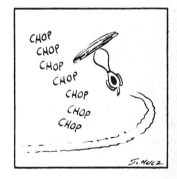

MA'AM?

HOW COME WE'VE ONLY BEEN STUDYING ABOUT MEN IN HISTORY?

AREN'T WE GOING TO STUDY ABOUT WOMEN?

I HAD A GRANDMOTHER WHO WAS KIND OF CUTE!

MY GRANDMOTHER HELPED TO MAKE THIS COUNTRY GREAT!

DURING WORLD WAR II, SHE WORKED AS A RIVETER, AND WROTE LETTERS TO SEVENTEEN SERVICEMEN!

TALK ABOUT WOMEN IN HISTORY...

LET'S HEAR IT FOR MY GRANDMOTHER!!

MY GRANDMOTHER LOVED TO DANCE

EVERY SATURDAY NIGHT SHE AND HER FRIENDS WENT TO THIS LITTLE PLACE THAT HAD A JUKE BOX, AND A DANCE FLOOR AND SIX BOOTHS...

SHE WAS THE FIRST ONE TO CARVE THOSE IMMORTAL WORDS ON THE BACK OF ONE OF THE BOOTHS, "KILROY WAS HERE"

ACTUALLY, ALTHOUGH GRANDMA WAS A LOT OF FUN, SHE WASN'T VERY CREATIVE!

AND SO, WORLD WAR II CAME TO AN END...

MY GRANDMOTHER LEFT HER JOB IN THE DEFENSE PLANT, AND WENT TO WORK FOR THE TELEPHONE COMPANY...

WE NEED TO STUDY THE LIVES OF GREAT WOMEN LIKE MY GRANDMOTHER...TALK TO YOUR OWN GRANDMOTHER TODAY... ASK HER QUESTIONS...

YOU'LL FIND SHE KNOWS MORE THAN PEANUT BUTTER COOKIES! THANK YOU!

I GOT AN "A" ON MY REPORT ABOUT MY GRANDMOTHER!

MY TEACHER SAID IT GAVE A UNIQUE PICTURE OF LIFE DURING WORLD WAR II

WAS YOUR GRANDFATHER IN WORLD WAR II?

NO, BUT HE'S SEEN "VICTORY AT SEA" TWELVE TIMES!

IF WE EVER HAVE AN INK SHORTAGE, YOU'RE GONNA BE BLAMED!

THIS IS MY REPORT ON EMERALDS..CLEOPATRA OWNED LOTS OF EMERALDS BECAUSE SHE HAD HER OWN EMERALD MINE...

EMERALDS, UNLIKE OTHER STONES, APPEAR THE SAME COLOR IN ARTIFICIAL LIGHT AS IN SUNLIGHT...

AND THAT'S ALL I KNOW ABOUT EMERALDS

WHAT I COULD TELL YOU ABOUT CLEOPATRA, HOWEVER, WOULD MAKE YOUR HEAD SPIN!

YESTERDAY WE TALKED ABOUT EMERALDS...

TODAY MY REPORT IS ON THE MOONSTONE... THIS IS A MYSTERIOUS GEM SURROUNDED BY MANY INTRIGUING LEGENDS...

IT HAS BEEN SAID THAT THE MOONSTONE CAN BANISH FEARS

FRANKLY, HOWEVER, I WOULDN'T COUNT ON IT IF YOU'RE ABOUT TO GET MUGGED

MOONSTONES COME FROM CEYLON

THEY ARE CUT IN THE SHAPE OF A DOME TO ACCENT THE PLAY OF LIGHT

THEY SAY THIS MAKES THE MOONSTONE LOOK LIKE A RAINDROP SEEN THROUGH THE MIST AT EARLY DAWN

I WOULDN'T KNOW BECAUSE I NEVER GET UP THAT EARLY...

THIS CONCLUDES MY REPORT ON GEMS AND JEWELRY... ARE THERE ANY QUESTIONS?

YES, YOU IN THE BACK ROW...YOUR QUESTION, PLEASE

NO, YOU SHOULD NOT WEAR YOUR JEWELRY IF YOU ARE GOING TO SLIDE INTO SECOND BASE

SEEING THE STUPID TREND THAT THESE QUESTIONS ARE ABOUT TO TAKE, I WILL NOW SIT DOWN!

YES, MA'AM? YOU WANT ME TO WORK OUT THE PROBLEM AT THE BOARD?

WELL, LET'S SEE.. WE HAVE THESE NUMBERS HERE, DON'T WE?

4,678
X 52

THESE ARE NICE NUMBERS, MA'AM..

4,678
X 52

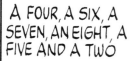
A FOUR, A SIX, A SEVEN, AN EIGHT, A FIVE AND A TWO

OH, YES, AND WE ALSO HAVE AN X ...

4,6
X

WELL, THE PROBLEM SEEMS TO BE TO TRY TO FIND OUT WHAT THIS X IS DOING AMONG ALL THESE NUMBERS...

IS HE AN OUTSIDER? WAS HE INVITED TO JOIN THE GROUP? IT'S AN INTERESTING QUESTION...

4,6
X

LET'S FIND OUT WHAT THE REST OF THE CLASS THINKS... YOU THERE, IN THE THIRD ROW...WHAT DO YOU THINK ABOUT THIS? SPEAK UP!

MA'AM?

RATS! THREE MORE MINUTES AND THE BELL WOULD HAVE RUNG!

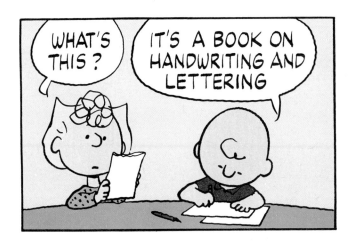

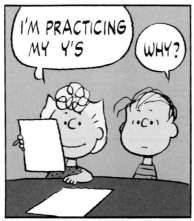

YOU KNOW WHAT I AM, MARCIE? I'M A WEED!

THE WORLD IS FILLED WITH BEAUTIFUL PLANTS AND FLOWERS, BUT I'M JUST AN UGLY WEED

I'M A POOR UGLY WEED TRYING TO PUSH HER WAY UP THROUGH THE SIDEWALK OF LIFE!

THAT'S A GREAT METAPHOR, SIR

DID YOU KNOW THAT WEEDS HAVE A WIDE TOLERANCE FOR ENVIRONMENTAL CONDITIONS AND THE RARE ABILITY TO EXPLOIT RECENTLY DISTURBED TERRAIN?

WHAT IN THE WORLD DOES THAT MEAN?

YOU CAN ROLL WITH THE PUNCHES, SIR!

BY GOLLY, MARCIE, I THINK YOU'RE RIGHT...

I'VE GOT MY CONFIDENCE BACK, MA'AM! ASK ME ANYTHING! GIVE ME YOUR BEST SHOT!!

I'LL BET THE PRINCIPAL WOULD BE SURPRISED TO FIND A WEED GROWING IN FRONT OF HIS OFFICE...

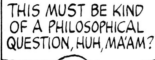

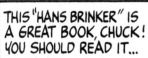

I NEED TO TALK TO SOMEONE WHO KNOWS WHAT IT'S LIKE TO FEEL LIKE A FOOL

SOMEONE WHO KNOWS WHAT IT'S LIKE TO BE HUMILIATED...

SOMEONE WHO'S BEEN DISGRACED, BEATEN AND DEGRADED.... SOMEONE WHO'S BEEN THERE...

WHAT DO YOU HAVE THERE, SIR?

IT'S A BOOK ON FIRST AID, MARCIE

HERE'S THE CHAPTER I WAS LOOKING FOR...

"WHAT TO DO IN CASE OF STUPIDITY"

I KNOW, MA'AM! I KNOW!

THE ANSWER IS, "THE WHOLE WORLD"

IT ISN'T? SORRY, MA'AM

I THOUGHT FOR SURE THE ANSWER WOULD BE IN THERE SOME PLACE

I HAVE IT ALL FIGURED OUT, MARCIE...

THE WAY I SEE IT, THERE SEEM TO BE MORE QUESTIONS THAN THERE ARE ANSWERS

SO?

SO TRY TO BE THE ONE WHO ASKS THE QUESTIONS!

THIS IS MY REPORT ON THE PAST

THE PAST HAS ALWAYS INTERESTED PEOPLE

I MUST ADMIT, HOWEVER, THAT I DON'T KNOW MUCH ABOUT IT

I WASN'T HERE WHEN IT HAPPENED

ME?

YES, MA'AM... I AGREE..

THE ANSWER REALLY LIES DEEP WITHIN THE HEARTS OF ALL OF US

THE ANSWER IS ACTUALLY A PART OF OUR HERITAGE, OUR CULTURE, OUR WHOLE WAY OF LIVING...

THE ANSWER IS THE WAY EACH OF US CONTRIBUTES A LITTLE SOMETHING TO OUR FUTURE!

THAT WAS VERY GOOD, SIR

THANK YOU, MARCIE

EXCEPT THE ANSWER WAS "TWELVE"!

SEVEN, EIGHT, NINE, TEN! HA!!

"7+3=10"...THAT'S AN EASY ONE, MARCIE...

ANYTHING WITH A "3" IS EASY BECAUSE YOU JUST TAKE THE FIRST NUMBER AND THEN COUNT THE LITTLE POINTY THINGS ON THE "3," AND YOU HAVE THE ANSWER!

WHAT ABOUT "TWELVES," SIR?

NO ONE CAN BE EXPECTED TO ANSWER A PROBLEM WITH A "TWELVE" IN IT!

IF A PROBLEM HAS REALLY BIG NUMBERS IN IT, THE ANSWER IS ALWAYS "ONE MILLION"!

MATH IS LIKE LEARNING A FOREIGN LANGUAGE, MARCIE...NO MATTER WHAT YOU SAY, IT'S GOING TO BE WRONG ANYWAY!

LET'S SEE..."NINE PLUS THREE"...I TAKE THE NINE AND COUNT THE LITTLE POINTY THINGS ON THE THREE...TEN, ELEVEN, TWELVE...THE ANSWER IS "TWELVE"... HA!!

WOW!

LOOK, MARCIE, LOOK!

I GOT AN "A" ON MY FINAL REPORT CARD!

I'VE NEVER GOTTEN AN "A" BEFORE! HOW ABOUT THAT?

ALL I SEE ARE A BUNCH OF "D MINUSES," SIR

LOOK AT THE TOP, MARCIE.. IT'S RIGHT THERE AT THE TOP...

IT SAYS,"REPORT CARD," SIR..THIS "A" IS JUST PART OF THE WORD...

RATS! NOT GETTING AN "A" WHEN YOU THINK YOU DID IS LIKE LOSING A TIE BREAKER..

AHEM!

THIS IS MY REPORT ON "HANS BRINKER OR THE SILVER SKATES"

THE MAIN EMPHASIS OF MY REPORT WILL DEAL WITH THE STRANGE SECTION THAT BEGINS ON PAGE SEVENTY-TWO..

HERE WE HAVE THE STORY OF THE BOY WHO SAVED THE CITY BY PLACING HIS FINGER IN THE HOLE OF THE DIKE...

THUS, HE STOPPED THE LEAK THAT WOULD HAVE FLOODED THE CITY...HE WAS A HERO!

HOWEVER, WHAT IF THE BOY LOST THE USE OF HIS FINGER? COULD THE DOCTOR HAVE BEEN SUED FOR IMPROPER DIAGNOSIS?

AND WHAT IF THE BOY'S FAMILY BROUGHT A PERSONAL INJURY ACTION AGAINST THE CITY FOR FAILING TO PROPERLY MAINTAIN THE DIKE?

HAS ANYONE EVER THOUGHT OF THIS? ALL RIGHT, THEN, SUPPOSE WE..

MA'AM?

⁂ SIGH ⁂ ANOTHER D MINUS..

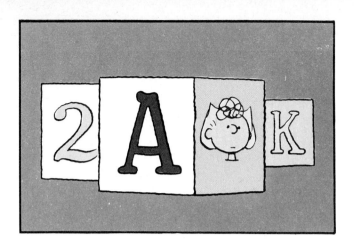

YES, MA'AM.. MORE THAN READY...

THEY'RE GONNA LOVE THIS, MARCIE!

THIS IS MY REPORT ON "WHAT I DID THIS SUMMER"... AT THE CONCLUSION, I WILL ANSWER QUESTIONS..

ONE DAY LATE IN THE SUMMER, I WAS LYING IN A MEADOW, WHEN SUDDENLY, A BUTTERFLY LANDED ON MY NOSE!

HA HA HA H
HA HA HA
HA HA HA

WELL, I DIDN'T WANT TO BRUSH IT AWAY BECAUSE I MIGHT HURT IT...

AFTER A WHILE I MUST HAVE DOZED OFF.. WHEN I OPENED MY EYES, THE BUTTERFLY WAS GONE!

YOU'LL NEVER GUESS WHAT HAPPENED... IT HAD TURNED INTO AN ANGEL, AND FLOWN AWAY!

HA HA HA
HA HA HA
HA HA

WELL, THIS WAS OBVIOUSLY A MIRACLE! I HAD BEEN CHOSEN TO BRING A MESSAGE TO THE WORLD!

WHAT WAS THIS MESSAGE I WAS TO BRING TO THE WORLD? AFTER MUCH THOUGHT, I DECIDED IT WAS THIS, "A FOUL BALL HIT BEHIND THIRD BASE IS THE SHORTSTOP'S PLAY!"

HAHAHA
HA HA
HA HA

MA'AM, IF IT'S OKAY WITH YOU, I'LL TAKE THE QUESTIONS AFTER SCHOOL OUT IN THE ALLEY BEHIND THE GYM!

"NINE FORTY-FIVE..FIRST SIGNS OF DROWSINESS"

I'M MAKING A STUDY OF YOUR IN-SCHOOL SLEEPING HABITS, SIR

BACKWARDS SEEMS OKAY...

Z

FORWARDS ALSO SEEMS OKAY

Z

KLUNK!

SIDEWAYS NEEDS A LITTLE WORK

PRINTED IN BELGIUM BY
proost
INTERNATIONAL BOOK PRODUCTION